DUE DATE

GW00374781

CONTENTS

mother

NAME			
D.O.B		Age	
Eye Color		Skin Color	
Height		Weight	
Blood Group		Occupation	

Things I Enjoy Doing	
Relaxation Methods	
What I Am Looking Forward To	
What I Am Worried About	

NOTES

	Me	My Mother	My father	NOTES
High Blood Pressure				
Diabetes				
Stroke				
High Cholesterol				
Glaucoma				
Epilepsy				
Asthma				
Obesity				
Allergies				
Cancer (type)				
Hearing Loss				
Alcohol Misuse				
Drug Misuse				
Kidney Problems				

father

NAME			
D.O.B		Age	
Eye Color		Skin Color	
Height		Weight	
Blood Group		Occupation	

Things I Enjoy Doing	
Relaxation Methods	
What I Am Looking Forward To	
What I Am Worried About	

NOTES

	Dad	My Mother	My father	NOTES
High Blood Pressure				
Diabetes				
Stroke				
High Cholesterol				
Glaucoma				
Epilepsy				
Asthma				
Obesity				
Allergies				
Cancer (type)				
Hearing Loss				
Alcohol Misuse				
Drug Misuse				
Kidney Problems				

contact details

EMERGENCY CONTACT 1

NAME	
RELATIONSHIP	
CONTACT NUMBER	
ADDRESS	
NOTES	

EMERGENCY CONTACT 2

NAME	
RELATIONSHIP	
CONTACT NUMBER	
ADDRESS	
NOTES	

INSURANCE DETAILS

COMPANY	
POLICY DETAILS	
COVER DETAILS	
ADDRESS	
CONTACT NO.	
CONTACT PERSON	
EMAIL	
WEBSITE	

6

HEALTH CARE DETAILS

MIDWIFE	
NAME:	
ADDRESS:	
PHONE NUMBER:	

DOCTOR	
NAME:	
ADDRESS:	
PHONE NUMBER:	

CONSULTANTS	
NAME:	
DETAILS:	
ADDRESS:	
PHONE NUMBER:	

BABY CLINIC	
NAME:	
ADDRESS:	
PHONE NUMBER:	

ULTRASOUND	
NAME:	
ADDRESS:	
PHONE NUMBER:	

MATERNITY WARD	
NAME:	
DETAILS:	
ADDRESS:	
PHONE NUMBER:	

NAME:
ADDRESS:

PHONE NUMBER:

NAME:
ADDRESS:

PHONE NUMBER:

NAME:
DETAILS:
ADDRESS:

PHONE NUMBER:

NAME:
ADDRESS:

PHONE NUMBER:

NAME:
ADDRESS:

PHONE NUMBER:

NAME:
DETAILS:
ADDRESS:

PHONE NUMBER:

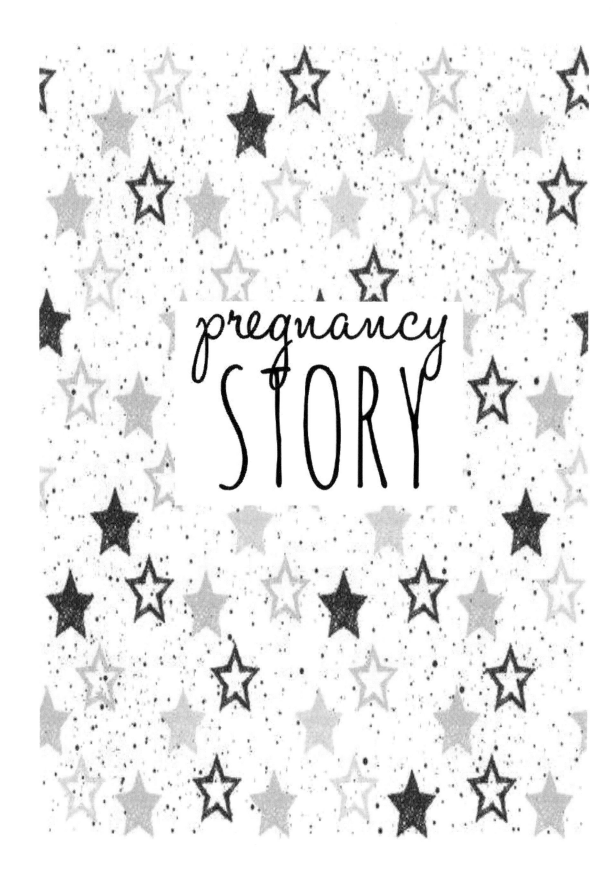

pregnancy STORY

Example Information:
- How long were you trying for a baby?
- Where were you when you found out you were pregnant?
- Who was the first person you told?

BIRTHING PLAN

Who I want to be at the birth/ My Birthing Partner						
Duration Present	At The Start		Throughout		At the End	
Midwifes Name						
Midwifes Contact Number						

Pain Relief Required?	None		As little as possible	
	As Much as possible		Will Decide at the time	

Type of Pain Relief	Entonox (Gas & Air)		Pethidine	
	Epidural		TENS	
	Birthing Pool		Don't Mind	
	Natural Method		Details:	

What Position Would You Like To Give Birth In?	In Bed		Squatting		Standing	
	Kneeling		Birth Ball		Water	
	Birthing Stool		Side Laying		Other:	

Atmosphere In The Room					
Student Midwifes In The Room?	Yes		No		Maybe	
Who can make medical decisions if you are unable to?					

OTHER BIRTH/ DELIVERY PLAN

_____
_____
_____
_____
_____
_____

POST DELIVERY PLAN

_____
_____
_____
_____
_____
_____

WHEN BABY IS DELIVERED

Hold Baby To Skin Immediately	Yes		No		Other	
Who Will Cut The Umbilical Cord?					
Keep The Placenta?	Yes		No		Other	

NOTES

_____
_____
_____
_____
_____
_____
_____

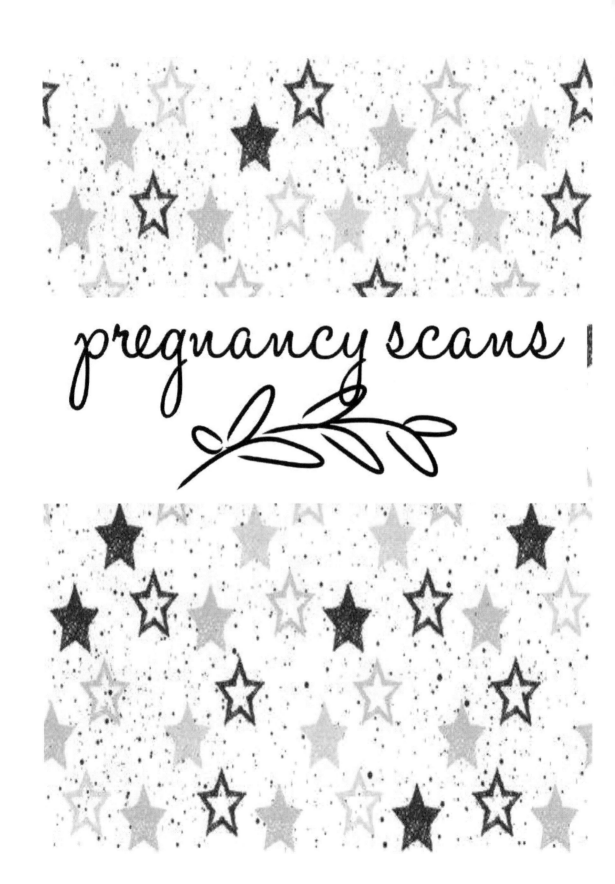

pregnancy scans

PREGNANCY WEEK		DATE	
VISIT NUMBER		SCAN LOCATION	

Current Length Of Baby	
Current Weight Of Baby	
Baby Heart Rate	
Blood Pressure	
Any Changes From Previous Visit	
Other Tests	
Medication Prescribed	
Other information	

BABY SCAN

PREGNANCY WEEK		DATE	
VISIT NUMBER		SCAN LOCATION	

Current Length Of Baby	
Current Weight Of Baby	
Baby Heart Rate	
Blood Pressure	
Any Changes From Previous Visit	
Other Tests	
Medication Prescribed	
Other information	

PREGNANCY WEEK		DATE	
VISIT NUMBER		SCAN LOCATION	

Current Length Of Baby	
Current Weight Of Baby	
Baby Heart Rate	
Blood Pressure	
Any Changes From Previous Visit	
Other Tests	
Medication Prescribed	
Other information	

BABY SCAN

PREGNANCY WEEK		DATE	
VISIT NUMBER		SCAN LOCATION	

Current Length Of Baby	
Current Weight Of Baby	
Baby Heart Rate	
Blood Pressure	
Any Changes From Previous Visit	
Other Tests	
Medication Prescribed	
Other information	

PREGNANCY WEEK		DATE	
VISIT NUMBER		**SCAN LOCATION**	

Current Length Of Baby	
Current Weight Of Baby	
Baby Heart Rate	
Blood Pressure	

Any Changes From Previous Visit	
Other Tests	
Medication Prescribed	
Other information	

BABY SCAN

PREGNANCY WEEK		DATE	
VISIT NUMBER		SCAN LOCATION	

Current Length Of Baby	
Current Weight Of Baby	
Baby Heart Rate	
Blood Pressure	
Any Changes From Previous Visit	
Other Tests	
Medication Prescribed	
Other information	

PREGNANCY WEEK		DATE	
VISIT NUMBER		SCAN LOCATION	

Current Length Of Baby	
Current Weight Of Baby	
Baby Heart Rate	
Blood Pressure	
Any Changes From Previous Visit	
Other Tests	
Medication Prescribed	
Other information	

BABY SCAN

PREGNANCY WEEK		DATE	
VISIT NUMBER		SCAN LOCATION	

Current Length Of Baby	
Current Weight Of Baby	
Baby Heart Rate	
Blood Pressure	
Any Changes From Previous Visit	
Other Tests	
Medication Prescribed	
Other information	

PREGNANCY WEEK		DATE	
VISIT NUMBER		**SCAN LOCATION**	

Current Length Of Baby	
Current Weight Of Baby	
Baby Heart Rate	
Blood Pressure	
Any Changes From Previous Visit	
Other Tests	
Medication Prescribed	
Other information	

prenatal learning

DATE & TIME	LOCATION	CLASS NAME	RATING

LITERATURE TO READ

BOOK/ MAGAZINE	✓

BLOGS	✓

VIDEO	✓

NOTES

NAME SUGGESTIONS

NAME	MEANING	CHOOSEN BY

PREGNANCY
milestones

1st TRIMESTER MILESTONES	DATE/ MONTH
Positive Pregnancy Test	
Told My Partner	
First Prenatal Visit	
Morning Sickness	
First Food Evasion	
First Craving	
Heard My Baby's Heartbeat	

2nd TRIMESTER MILESTONES	DATE/ MONTH
Made The Big Announcement	
Saw My Baby	
Heard My Baby's Heart Beat	
Felt My Baby Move	
Purchased Maternity Clothes	
Found Out The Gender	

3rd TRIMESTER MILESTONES	DATE/ MONTH
Saw My Baby Move	
Couldn't See My Feet	
Started Counting Down	
Started Maternity Leave	
First Contraction	

weekly
PREGNANCY DIARY

week [   ] **date** [   ]

MONDAY

I AM FEELING....	
CRAVINGS	
SYMPTOMS	
CHANGES NOTED	

TUESDAY

I AM FEELING....	
CRAVINGS	
SYMPTOMS	
CHANGES NOTED	

WEDNESDAY

I AM FEELING....	
CRAVINGS	
SYMPTOMS	
CHANGES NOTED	

THURSDAY

I AM FEELING....	
CRAVINGS	
SYMPTOMS	
CHANGES NOTED	

FRIDAY

I AM FEELING....	
CRAVINGS	
SYMPTOMS	
CHANGES NOTED	

SATURDAY	
I AM FEELING....	
CRAVINGS	
SYMPTOMS	
CHANGES NOTED	

SUNDAY	
I AM FEELING....	
CRAVINGS	
SYMPTOMS	
CHANGES NOTED	

MY BUMP

week [   ]   *date* [   ]

MONDAY

I AM FEELING....

CRAVINGS

SYMPTOMS

CHANGES NOTED

TUESDAY

I AM FEELING....

CRAVINGS

SYMPTOMS

CHANGES NOTED

WEDNESDAY

I AM FEELING....

CRAVINGS

SYMPTOMS

CHANGES NOTED

THURSDAY

I AM FEELING....

CRAVINGS

SYMPTOMS

CHANGES NOTED

FRIDAY

I AM FEELING....

CRAVINGS

SYMPTOMS

CHANGES NOTED

SATURDAY	
I AM FEELING....	
CRAVINGS	
SYMPTOMS	
CHANGES NOTED	

SUNDAY	
I AM FEELING....	
CRAVINGS	
SYMPTOMS	
CHANGES NOTED	

MY BUMP

week [ ] *date* [ ]

MONDAY

I AM FEELING....	
CRAVINGS	
SYMPTOMS	
CHANGES NOTED	

TUESDAY

I AM FEELING....	
CRAVINGS	
SYMPTOMS	
CHANGES NOTED	

WEDNESDAY

I AM FEELING....	
CRAVINGS	
SYMPTOMS	
CHANGES NOTED	

THURSDAY

I AM FEELING....	
CRAVINGS	
SYMPTOMS	
CHANGES NOTED	

FRIDAY

I AM FEELING....	
CRAVINGS	
SYMPTOMS	
CHANGES NOTED	

SATURDAY	
I AM FEELING....	
CRAVINGS	
SYMPTOMS	
CHANGES NOTED	

SUNDAY	
I AM FEELING....	
CRAVINGS	
SYMPTOMS	
CHANGES NOTED	

MY BUMP

week ⬚   date ⬚

MONDAY

I AM FEELING....

CRAVINGS

SYMPTOMS

CHANGES NOTED

TUESDAY

I AM FEELING....

CRAVINGS

SYMPTOMS

CHANGES NOTED

WEDNESDAY

I AM FEELING....

CRAVINGS

SYMPTOMS

CHANGES NOTED

THURSDAY

I AM FEELING....

CRAVINGS

SYMPTOMS

CHANGES NOTED

FRIDAY

I AM FEELING....

CRAVINGS

SYMPTOMS

CHANGES NOTED

SATURDAY	
I AM FEELING....	
CRAVINGS	
SYMPTOMS	
CHANGES NOTED	

SUNDAY	
I AM FEELING....	
CRAVINGS	
SYMPTOMS	
CHANGES NOTED	

MY BUMP

week [　　　]   *date* [　　　　　　　]

MONDAY

I AM FEELING....	
CRAVINGS	
SYMPTOMS	
CHANGES NOTED	

TUESDAY

I AM FEELING....	
CRAVINGS	
SYMPTOMS	
CHANGES NOTED	

WEDNESDAY

I AM FEELING....	
CRAVINGS	
SYMPTOMS	
CHANGES NOTED	

THURSDAY

I AM FEELING....	
CRAVINGS	
SYMPTOMS	
CHANGES NOTED	

FRIDAY

I AM FEELING....	
CRAVINGS	
SYMPTOMS	
CHANGES NOTED	

SATURDAY	
I AM FEELING....	
CRAVINGS	
SYMPTOMS	
CHANGES NOTED	

SUNDAY	
I AM FEELING....	
CRAVINGS	
SYMPTOMS	
CHANGES NOTED	

MY BUMP

week [   ] date [   ]

MONDAY

I AM FEELING....

CRAVINGS

SYMPTOMS

CHANGES NOTED

TUESDAY

I AM FEELING....

CRAVINGS

SYMPTOMS

CHANGES NOTED

WEDNESDAY

I AM FEELING....

CRAVINGS

SYMPTOMS

CHANGES NOTED

THURSDAY

I AM FEELING....

CRAVINGS

SYMPTOMS

CHANGES NOTED

FRIDAY

I AM FEELING....

CRAVINGS

SYMPTOMS

CHANGES NOTED

SATURDAY	
I AM FEELING....	
CRAVINGS	
SYMPTOMS	
CHANGES NOTED	

SUNDAY	
I AM FEELING....	
CRAVINGS	
SYMPTOMS	
CHANGES NOTED	

MY BUMP

week ⸤_____⸥   *date* ⸤_____⸥

MONDAY

I AM FEELING….	
CRAVINGS	
SYMPTOMS	
CHANGES NOTED	

TUESDAY

I AM FEELING….	
CRAVINGS	
SYMPTOMS	
CHANGES NOTED	

WEDNESDAY

I AM FEELING….	
CRAVINGS	
SYMPTOMS	
CHANGES NOTED	

THURSDAY

I AM FEELING….	
CRAVINGS	
SYMPTOMS	
CHANGES NOTED	

FRIDAY

I AM FEELING….	
CRAVINGS	
SYMPTOMS	
CHANGES NOTED	

SATURDAY	
I AM FEELING....	
CRAVINGS	
SYMPTOMS	
CHANGES NOTED	

SUNDAY	
I AM FEELING....	
CRAVINGS	
SYMPTOMS	
CHANGES NOTED	

MY BUMP

week ⬚ *date* ⬚

MONDAY

I AM FEELING....

CRAVINGS

SYMPTOMS

CHANGES NOTED

TUESDAY

I AM FEELING....

CRAVINGS

SYMPTOMS

CHANGES NOTED

WEDNESDAY

I AM FEELING....

CRAVINGS

SYMPTOMS

CHANGES NOTED

THURSDAY

I AM FEELING....

CRAVINGS

SYMPTOMS

CHANGES NOTED

FRIDAY

I AM FEELING....

CRAVINGS

SYMPTOMS

CHANGES NOTED

SATURDAY	
I AM FEELING....	
CRAVINGS	
SYMPTOMS	
CHANGES NOTED	

SUNDAY	
I AM FEELING....	
CRAVINGS	
SYMPTOMS	
CHANGES NOTED	

MY BUMP

week [_____]   date [_____]

MONDAY

I AM FEELING....

CRAVINGS

SYMPTOMS

CHANGES NOTED

TUESDAY

I AM FEELING....

CRAVINGS

SYMPTOMS

CHANGES NOTED

WEDNESDAY

I AM FEELING....

CRAVINGS

SYMPTOMS

CHANGES NOTED

THURSDAY

I AM FEELING....

CRAVINGS

SYMPTOMS

CHANGES NOTED

FRIDAY

I AM FEELING....

CRAVINGS

SYMPTOMS

CHANGES NOTED

SATURDAY	
I AM FEELING....	
CRAVINGS	
SYMPTOMS	
CHANGES NOTED	

SUNDAY	
I AM FEELING....	
CRAVINGS	
SYMPTOMS	
CHANGES NOTED	

MY BUMP

week [ ]   date [ ]

MONDAY	
I AM FEELING....	
CRAVINGS	
SYMPTOMS	
CHANGES NOTED	

TUESDAY	
I AM FEELING....	
CRAVINGS	
SYMPTOMS	
CHANGES NOTED	

WEDNESDAY	
I AM FEELING....	
CRAVINGS	
SYMPTOMS	
CHANGES NOTED	

THURSDAY	
I AM FEELING....	
CRAVINGS	
SYMPTOMS	
CHANGES NOTED	

FRIDAY	
I AM FEELING....	
CRAVINGS	
SYMPTOMS	
CHANGES NOTED	

SATURDAY	
I AM FEELING....	
CRAVINGS	
SYMPTOMS	
CHANGES NOTED	

SUNDAY	
I AM FEELING....	
CRAVINGS	
SYMPTOMS	
CHANGES NOTED	

MY BUMP

week [ ]   date [ ]

MONDAY

I AM FEELING....

CRAVINGS

SYMPTOMS

CHANGES NOTED

TUESDAY

I AM FEELING....

CRAVINGS

SYMPTOMS

CHANGES NOTED

WEDNESDAY

I AM FEELING....

CRAVINGS

SYMPTOMS

CHANGES NOTED

THURSDAY

I AM FEELING....

CRAVINGS

SYMPTOMS

CHANGES NOTED

FRIDAY

I AM FEELING....

CRAVINGS

SYMPTOMS

CHANGES NOTED

SATURDAY	
I AM FEELING....	
CRAVINGS	
SYMPTOMS	
CHANGES NOTED	

SUNDAY	
I AM FEELING....	
CRAVINGS	
SYMPTOMS	
CHANGES NOTED	

MY BUMP

week ☐   date ☐

MONDAY

I AM FEELING....	
CRAVINGS	
SYMPTOMS	
CHANGES NOTED	

TUESDAY

I AM FEELING....	
CRAVINGS	
SYMPTOMS	
CHANGES NOTED	

WEDNESDAY

I AM FEELING....	
CRAVINGS	
SYMPTOMS	
CHANGES NOTED	

THURSDAY

I AM FEELING....	
CRAVINGS	
SYMPTOMS	
CHANGES NOTED	

FRIDAY

I AM FEELING....	
CRAVINGS	
SYMPTOMS	
CHANGES NOTED	

SATURDAY	
I AM FEELING....	
CRAVINGS	
SYMPTOMS	
CHANGES NOTED	

SUNDAY	
I AM FEELING....	
CRAVINGS	
SYMPTOMS	
CHANGES NOTED	

MY BUMP

week [ ] date [ ]

MONDAY

I AM FEELING....	
CRAVINGS	
SYMPTOMS	
CHANGES NOTED	

TUESDAY

I AM FEELING....	
CRAVINGS	
SYMPTOMS	
CHANGES NOTED	

WEDNESDAY

I AM FEELING....	
CRAVINGS	
SYMPTOMS	
CHANGES NOTED	

THURSDAY

I AM FEELING....	
CRAVINGS	
SYMPTOMS	
CHANGES NOTED	

FRIDAY

I AM FEELING....	
CRAVINGS	
SYMPTOMS	
CHANGES NOTED	

SATURDAY	
I AM FEELING....	
CRAVINGS	
SYMPTOMS	
CHANGES NOTED	

SUNDAY	
I AM FEELING....	
CRAVINGS	
SYMPTOMS	
CHANGES NOTED	

MY BUMP

week [ ]   date [ ]

MONDAY

I AM FEELING....	
CRAVINGS	
SYMPTOMS	
CHANGES NOTED	

TUESDAY

I AM FEELING....	
CRAVINGS	
SYMPTOMS	
CHANGES NOTED	

WEDNESDAY

I AM FEELING....	
CRAVINGS	
SYMPTOMS	
CHANGES NOTED	

THURSDAY

I AM FEELING....	
CRAVINGS	
SYMPTOMS	
CHANGES NOTED	

FRIDAY

I AM FEELING....	
CRAVINGS	
SYMPTOMS	
CHANGES NOTED	

SATURDAY	
I AM FEELING....	
CRAVINGS	
SYMPTOMS	
CHANGES NOTED	

SUNDAY	
I AM FEELING....	
CRAVINGS	
SYMPTOMS	
CHANGES NOTED	

MY BUMP

week ☐ date ☐

MONDAY

I AM FEELING....	
CRAVINGS	
SYMPTOMS	
CHANGES NOTED	

TUESDAY

I AM FEELING....	
CRAVINGS	
SYMPTOMS	
CHANGES NOTED	

WEDNESDAY

I AM FEELING....	
CRAVINGS	
SYMPTOMS	
CHANGES NOTED	

THURSDAY

I AM FEELING....	
CRAVINGS	
SYMPTOMS	
CHANGES NOTED	

FRIDAY

I AM FEELING....	
CRAVINGS	
SYMPTOMS	
CHANGES NOTED	

SATURDAY	
I AM FEELING....	
CRAVINGS	
SYMPTOMS	
CHANGES NOTED	

SUNDAY	
I AM FEELING....	
CRAVINGS	
SYMPTOMS	
CHANGES NOTED	

MY BUMP

week [ ]   date [ ]

MONDAY	
I AM FEELING....	
CRAVINGS	
SYMPTOMS	
CHANGES NOTED	

TUESDAY	
I AM FEELING....	
CRAVINGS	
SYMPTOMS	
CHANGES NOTED	

WEDNESDAY	
I AM FEELING....	
CRAVINGS	
SYMPTOMS	
CHANGES NOTED	

THURSDAY	
I AM FEELING....	
CRAVINGS	
SYMPTOMS	
CHANGES NOTED	

FRIDAY	
I AM FEELING....	
CRAVINGS	
SYMPTOMS	
CHANGES NOTED	

SATURDAY	
I AM FEELING....	
CRAVINGS	
SYMPTOMS	
CHANGES NOTED	

SUNDAY	
I AM FEELING....	
CRAVINGS	
SYMPTOMS	
CHANGES NOTED	

MY BUMP

week [ ]   date [ ]

MONDAY

I AM FEELING....

CRAVINGS

SYMPTOMS

CHANGES NOTED

TUESDAY

I AM FEELING....

CRAVINGS

SYMPTOMS

CHANGES NOTED

WEDNESDAY

I AM FEELING....

CRAVINGS

SYMPTOMS

CHANGES NOTED

THURSDAY

I AM FEELING....

CRAVINGS

SYMPTOMS

CHANGES NOTED

FRIDAY

I AM FEELING....

CRAVINGS

SYMPTOMS

CHANGES NOTED

SATURDAY	
I AM FEELING....	
CRAVINGS	
SYMPTOMS	
CHANGES NOTED	

SUNDAY	
I AM FEELING....	
CRAVINGS	
SYMPTOMS	
CHANGES NOTED	

MY BUMP

week [   ]   _date_ [   ]

MONDAY

I AM FEELING....

CRAVINGS

SYMPTOMS

CHANGES NOTED

TUESDAY

I AM FEELING....

CRAVINGS

SYMPTOMS

CHANGES NOTED

WEDNESDAY

I AM FEELING....

CRAVINGS

SYMPTOMS

CHANGES NOTED

THURSDAY

I AM FEELING....

CRAVINGS

SYMPTOMS

CHANGES NOTED

FRIDAY

I AM FEELING....

CRAVINGS

SYMPTOMS

CHANGES NOTED

SATURDAY	
I AM FEELING....	
CRAVINGS	
SYMPTOMS	
CHANGES NOTED	

SUNDAY	
I AM FEELING....	
CRAVINGS	
SYMPTOMS	
CHANGES NOTED	

MY BUMP

week ___   date ___

MONDAY

I AM FEELING....

CRAVINGS

SYMPTOMS

CHANGES NOTED

TUESDAY

I AM FEELING....

CRAVINGS

SYMPTOMS

CHANGES NOTED

WEDNESDAY

I AM FEELING....

CRAVINGS

SYMPTOMS

CHANGES NOTED

THURSDAY

I AM FEELING....

CRAVINGS

SYMPTOMS

CHANGES NOTED

FRIDAY

I AM FEELING....

CRAVINGS

SYMPTOMS

CHANGES NOTED

SATURDAY	
I AM FEELING....	
CRAVINGS	
SYMPTOMS	
CHANGES NOTED	

SUNDAY	
I AM FEELING....	
CRAVINGS	
SYMPTOMS	
CHANGES NOTED	

MY BUMP

week [   ]   date [   ]

MONDAY

I AM FEELING....	
CRAVINGS	
SYMPTOMS	
CHANGES NOTED	

TUESDAY

I AM FEELING....	
CRAVINGS	
SYMPTOMS	
CHANGES NOTED	

WEDNESDAY

I AM FEELING....	
CRAVINGS	
SYMPTOMS	
CHANGES NOTED	

THURSDAY

I AM FEELING....	
CRAVINGS	
SYMPTOMS	
CHANGES NOTED	

FRIDAY

I AM FEELING....	
CRAVINGS	
SYMPTOMS	
CHANGES NOTED	

SATURDAY	
I AM FEELING....	
CRAVINGS	
SYMPTOMS	
CHANGES NOTED	

SUNDAY	
I AM FEELING....	
CRAVINGS	
SYMPTOMS	
CHANGES NOTED	

MY BUMP

week [ ]   date [ ]

MONDAY

I AM FEELING....

CRAVINGS

SYMPTOMS

CHANGES NOTED

TUESDAY

I AM FEELING....

CRAVINGS

SYMPTOMS

CHANGES NOTED

WEDNESDAY

I AM FEELING....

CRAVINGS

SYMPTOMS

CHANGES NOTED

THURSDAY

I AM FEELING....

CRAVINGS

SYMPTOMS

CHANGES NOTED

FRIDAY

I AM FEELING....

CRAVINGS

SYMPTOMS

CHANGES NOTED

SATURDAY	
I AM FEELING....	
CRAVINGS	
SYMPTOMS	
CHANGES NOTED	

SUNDAY	
I AM FEELING....	
CRAVINGS	
SYMPTOMS	
CHANGES NOTED	

MY BUMP

week [____]   date [_____]

MONDAY

I AM FEELING....	
CRAVINGS	
SYMPTOMS	
CHANGES NOTED	

TUESDAY

I AM FEELING....	
CRAVINGS	
SYMPTOMS	
CHANGES NOTED	

WEDNESDAY

I AM FEELING....	
CRAVINGS	
SYMPTOMS	
CHANGES NOTED	

THURSDAY

I AM FEELING....	
CRAVINGS	
SYMPTOMS	
CHANGES NOTED	

FRIDAY

I AM FEELING....	
CRAVINGS	
SYMPTOMS	
CHANGES NOTED	

SATURDAY	
I AM FEELING....	
CRAVINGS	
SYMPTOMS	
CHANGES NOTED	

SUNDAY	
I AM FEELING....	
CRAVINGS	
SYMPTOMS	
CHANGES NOTED	

MY BUMP

week ☐ *date* ☐

MONDAY	
I AM FEELING....	
CRAVINGS	
SYMPTOMS	
CHANGES NOTED	

TUESDAY	
I AM FEELING....	
CRAVINGS	
SYMPTOMS	
CHANGES NOTED	

WEDNESDAY	
I AM FEELING....	
CRAVINGS	
SYMPTOMS	
CHANGES NOTED	

THURSDAY	
I AM FEELING....	
CRAVINGS	
SYMPTOMS	
CHANGES NOTED	

FRIDAY	
I AM FEELING....	
CRAVINGS	
SYMPTOMS	
CHANGES NOTED	

SATURDAY	
I AM FEELING….	
CRAVINGS	
SYMPTOMS	
CHANGES NOTED	

SUNDAY	
I AM FEELING….	
CRAVINGS	
SYMPTOMS	
CHANGES NOTED	

MY BUMP

week ☐ date ☐

MONDAY

I AM FEELING....	
CRAVINGS	
SYMPTOMS	
CHANGES NOTED	

TUESDAY

I AM FEELING....	
CRAVINGS	
SYMPTOMS	
CHANGES NOTED	

WEDNESDAY

I AM FEELING....	
CRAVINGS	
SYMPTOMS	
CHANGES NOTED	

THURSDAY

I AM FEELING....	
CRAVINGS	
SYMPTOMS	
CHANGES NOTED	

FRIDAY

I AM FEELING....	
CRAVINGS	
SYMPTOMS	
CHANGES NOTED	

SATURDAY	
I AM FEELING....	
CRAVINGS	
SYMPTOMS	
CHANGES NOTED	

SUNDAY	
I AM FEELING....	
CRAVINGS	
SYMPTOMS	
CHANGES NOTED	

MY BUMP

week [ ] date [ ]

MONDAY

I AM FEELING....	
CRAVINGS	
SYMPTOMS	
CHANGES NOTED	

TUESDAY

I AM FEELING....	
CRAVINGS	
SYMPTOMS	
CHANGES NOTED	

WEDNESDAY

I AM FEELING....	
CRAVINGS	
SYMPTOMS	
CHANGES NOTED	

THURSDAY

I AM FEELING....	
CRAVINGS	
SYMPTOMS	
CHANGES NOTED	

FRIDAY

I AM FEELING....	
CRAVINGS	
SYMPTOMS	
CHANGES NOTED	

SATURDAY	
I AM FEELING....	
CRAVINGS	
SYMPTOMS	
CHANGES NOTED	

SUNDAY	
I AM FEELING....	
CRAVINGS	
SYMPTOMS	
CHANGES NOTED	

MY BUMP

week ☐   date ☐

MONDAY

I AM FEELING....

CRAVINGS
SYMPTOMS
CHANGES NOTED

TUESDAY

I AM FEELING....

CRAVINGS
SYMPTOMS
CHANGES NOTED

WEDNESDAY

I AM FEELING....

CRAVINGS
SYMPTOMS
CHANGES NOTED

THURSDAY

I AM FEELING....

CRAVINGS
SYMPTOMS
CHANGES NOTED

FRIDAY

I AM FEELING....

CRAVINGS
SYMPTOMS
CHANGES NOTED

SATURDAY	
I AM FEELING....	
CRAVINGS	
SYMPTOMS	
CHANGES NOTED	

SUNDAY	
I AM FEELING....	
CRAVINGS	
SYMPTOMS	
CHANGES NOTED	

MY BUMP

week ⬚ date ⬚

MONDAY

I AM FEELING....

CRAVINGS

SYMPTOMS

CHANGES NOTED

TUESDAY

I AM FEELING....

CRAVINGS

SYMPTOMS

CHANGES NOTED

WEDNESDAY

I AM FEELING....

CRAVINGS

SYMPTOMS

CHANGES NOTED

THURSDAY

I AM FEELING....

CRAVINGS

SYMPTOMS

CHANGES NOTED

FRIDAY

I AM FEELING....

CRAVINGS

SYMPTOMS

CHANGES NOTED

SATURDAY	
I AM FEELING....	
CRAVINGS	
SYMPTOMS	
CHANGES NOTED	

SUNDAY	
I AM FEELING....	
CRAVINGS	
SYMPTOMS	
CHANGES NOTED	

MY BUMP

week _____   date _____

MONDAY

I AM FEELING....	
CRAVINGS	
SYMPTOMS	
CHANGES NOTED	

TUESDAY

I AM FEELING....	
CRAVINGS	
SYMPTOMS	
CHANGES NOTED	

WEDNESDAY

I AM FEELING....	
CRAVINGS	
SYMPTOMS	
CHANGES NOTED	

THURSDAY

I AM FEELING....	
CRAVINGS	
SYMPTOMS	
CHANGES NOTED	

FRIDAY

I AM FEELING....	
CRAVINGS	
SYMPTOMS	
CHANGES NOTED	

SATURDAY	
I AM FEELING....	
CRAVINGS	
SYMPTOMS	
CHANGES NOTED	

SUNDAY	
I AM FEELING....	
CRAVINGS	
SYMPTOMS	
CHANGES NOTED	

MY BUMP

MONDAY

I AM FEELING....

CRAVINGS

SYMPTOMS

CHANGES NOTED

TUESDAY

I AM FEELING....

CRAVINGS

SYMPTOMS

CHANGES NOTED

WEDNESDAY

I AM FEELING....

CRAVINGS

SYMPTOMS

CHANGES NOTED

THURSDAY

I AM FEELING....

CRAVINGS

SYMPTOMS

CHANGES NOTED

FRIDAY

I AM FEELING....

CRAVINGS

SYMPTOMS

CHANGES NOTED

SATURDAY	
I AM FEELING....	
CRAVINGS	
SYMPTOMS	
CHANGES NOTED	

SUNDAY	
I AM FEELING....	
CRAVINGS	
SYMPTOMS	
CHANGES NOTED	

MY BUMP

week [____]   *date* [_____]

MONDAY

I AM FEELING....

CRAVINGS

SYMPTOMS

CHANGES NOTED

TUESDAY

I AM FEELING....

CRAVINGS

SYMPTOMS

CHANGES NOTED

WEDNESDAY

I AM FEELING....

CRAVINGS

SYMPTOMS

CHANGES NOTED

THURSDAY

I AM FEELING....

CRAVINGS

SYMPTOMS

CHANGES NOTED

FRIDAY

I AM FEELING....

CRAVINGS

SYMPTOMS

CHANGES NOTED

SATURDAY	
I AM FEELING....	
CRAVINGS	
SYMPTOMS	
CHANGES NOTED	

SUNDAY	
I AM FEELING....	
CRAVINGS	
SYMPTOMS	
CHANGES NOTED	

MY BUMP

week [   ]   *date* [   ]

MONDAY

I AM FEELING....

CRAVINGS
SYMPTOMS
CHANGES NOTED

TUESDAY

I AM FEELING....

CRAVINGS
SYMPTOMS
CHANGES NOTED

WEDNESDAY

I AM FEELING....

CRAVINGS
SYMPTOMS
CHANGES NOTED

THURSDAY

I AM FEELING....

CRAVINGS
SYMPTOMS
CHANGES NOTED

FRIDAY

I AM FEELING....

CRAVINGS
SYMPTOMS
CHANGES NOTED

SATURDAY	
I AM FEELING....	
CRAVINGS	
SYMPTOMS	
CHANGES NOTED	

SUNDAY	
I AM FEELING....	
CRAVINGS	
SYMPTOMS	
CHANGES NOTED	

MY BUMP

week [ ]   date [ ]

MONDAY

I AM FEELING....	
CRAVINGS	
SYMPTOMS	
CHANGES NOTED	

TUESDAY

I AM FEELING....	
CRAVINGS	
SYMPTOMS	
CHANGES NOTED	

WEDNESDAY

I AM FEELING....	
CRAVINGS	
SYMPTOMS	
CHANGES NOTED	

THURSDAY

I AM FEELING....	
CRAVINGS	
SYMPTOMS	
CHANGES NOTED	

FRIDAY

I AM FEELING....	
CRAVINGS	
SYMPTOMS	
CHANGES NOTED	

SATURDAY	
I AM FEELING....	
CRAVINGS	
SYMPTOMS	
CHANGES NOTED	

SUNDAY	
I AM FEELING....	
CRAVINGS	
SYMPTOMS	
CHANGES NOTED	

MY BUMP

week [ ] date [ ]

MONDAY

I AM FEELING....	
CRAVINGS	
SYMPTOMS	
CHANGES NOTED	

TUESDAY

I AM FEELING....	
CRAVINGS	
SYMPTOMS	
CHANGES NOTED	

WEDNESDAY

I AM FEELING....	
CRAVINGS	
SYMPTOMS	
CHANGES NOTED	

THURSDAY

I AM FEELING....	
CRAVINGS	
SYMPTOMS	
CHANGES NOTED	

FRIDAY

I AM FEELING....	
CRAVINGS	
SYMPTOMS	
CHANGES NOTED	

SATURDAY	
I AM FEELING....	
CRAVINGS	
SYMPTOMS	
CHANGES NOTED	

SUNDAY	
I AM FEELING....	
CRAVINGS	
SYMPTOMS	
CHANGES NOTED	

MY BUMP

week [ ]　　*date* [ ]

MONDAY

I AM FEELING....	
CRAVINGS	
SYMPTOMS	
CHANGES NOTED	

TUESDAY

I AM FEELING....	
CRAVINGS	
SYMPTOMS	
CHANGES NOTED	

WEDNESDAY

I AM FEELING....	
CRAVINGS	
SYMPTOMS	
CHANGES NOTED	

THURSDAY

I AM FEELING....	
CRAVINGS	
SYMPTOMS	
CHANGES NOTED	

FRIDAY

I AM FEELING....	
CRAVINGS	
SYMPTOMS	
CHANGES NOTED	

SATURDAY	
I AM FEELING....	
CRAVINGS	
SYMPTOMS	
CHANGES NOTED	

SUNDAY	
I AM FEELING....	
CRAVINGS	
SYMPTOMS	
CHANGES NOTED	

MY BUMP

week [   ]   _date_ [   ]

MONDAY

I AM FEELING....	
CRAVINGS	
SYMPTOMS	
CHANGES NOTED	

TUESDAY

I AM FEELING....	
CRAVINGS	
SYMPTOMS	
CHANGES NOTED	

WEDNESDAY

I AM FEELING....	
CRAVINGS	
SYMPTOMS	
CHANGES NOTED	

THURSDAY

I AM FEELING....	
CRAVINGS	
SYMPTOMS	
CHANGES NOTED	

FRIDAY

I AM FEELING....	
CRAVINGS	
SYMPTOMS	
CHANGES NOTED	

SATURDAY	
I AM FEELING....	
CRAVINGS	
SYMPTOMS	
CHANGES NOTED	

SUNDAY	
I AM FEELING....	
CRAVINGS	
SYMPTOMS	
CHANGES NOTED	

MY BUMP

week [ ]   date [ ]

MONDAY

I AM FEELING....	
CRAVINGS	
SYMPTOMS	
CHANGES NOTED	

TUESDAY

I AM FEELING....	
CRAVINGS	
SYMPTOMS	
CHANGES NOTED	

WEDNESDAY

I AM FEELING....	
CRAVINGS	
SYMPTOMS	
CHANGES NOTED	

THURSDAY

I AM FEELING....	
CRAVINGS	
SYMPTOMS	
CHANGES NOTED	

FRIDAY

I AM FEELING....	
CRAVINGS	
SYMPTOMS	
CHANGES NOTED	

SATURDAY	
I AM FEELING....	
CRAVINGS	
SYMPTOMS	
CHANGES NOTED	

SUNDAY	
I AM FEELING....	
CRAVINGS	
SYMPTOMS	
CHANGES NOTED	

MY BUMP

week [   ]   date [   ]

MONDAY

I AM FEELING....

CRAVINGS

SYMPTOMS

CHANGES NOTED

TUESDAY

I AM FEELING....

CRAVINGS

SYMPTOMS

CHANGES NOTED

WEDNESDAY

I AM FEELING....

CRAVINGS

SYMPTOMS

CHANGES NOTED

THURSDAY

I AM FEELING....

CRAVINGS

SYMPTOMS

CHANGES NOTED

FRIDAY

I AM FEELING....

CRAVINGS

SYMPTOMS

CHANGES NOTED

SATURDAY	
I AM FEELING....	
CRAVINGS	
SYMPTOMS	
CHANGES NOTED	

SUNDAY	
I AM FEELING....	
CRAVINGS	
SYMPTOMS	
CHANGES NOTED	

MY BUMP

week [   ]   *date* [   ]

MONDAY

I AM FEELING....

CRAVINGS
SYMPTOMS
CHANGES NOTED

TUESDAY

I AM FEELING....

CRAVINGS
SYMPTOMS
CHANGES NOTED

WEDNESDAY

I AM FEELING....

CRAVINGS
SYMPTOMS
CHANGES NOTED

THURSDAY

I AM FEELING....

CRAVINGS
SYMPTOMS
CHANGES NOTED

FRIDAY

I AM FEELING....

CRAVINGS
SYMPTOMS
CHANGES NOTED

SATURDAY	
I AM FEELING....	
CRAVINGS	
SYMPTOMS	
CHANGES NOTED	

SUNDAY	
I AM FEELING....	
CRAVINGS	
SYMPTOMS	
CHANGES NOTED	

MY BUMP

week [＿＿＿]   *date* [＿＿＿＿＿＿]

MONDAY

I AM FEELING....

CRAVINGS

SYMPTOMS

CHANGES NOTED

TUESDAY

I AM FEELING....

CRAVINGS

SYMPTOMS

CHANGES NOTED

WEDNESDAY

I AM FEELING....

CRAVINGS

SYMPTOMS

CHANGES NOTED

THURSDAY

I AM FEELING....

CRAVINGS

SYMPTOMS

CHANGES NOTED

FRIDAY

I AM FEELING....

CRAVINGS

SYMPTOMS

CHANGES NOTED

SATURDAY	
I AM FEELING....	
CRAVINGS	
SYMPTOMS	
CHANGES NOTED	

SUNDAY	
I AM FEELING....	
CRAVINGS	
SYMPTOMS	
CHANGES NOTED	

MY BUMP

week [ ]   *date* [ ]

MONDAY

I AM FEELING....	
CRAVINGS	
SYMPTOMS	
CHANGES NOTED	

TUESDAY

I AM FEELING....	
CRAVINGS	
SYMPTOMS	
CHANGES NOTED	

WEDNESDAY

I AM FEELING....	
CRAVINGS	
SYMPTOMS	
CHANGES NOTED	

THURSDAY

I AM FEELING....	
CRAVINGS	
SYMPTOMS	
CHANGES NOTED	

FRIDAY

I AM FEELING....	
CRAVINGS	
SYMPTOMS	
CHANGES NOTED	

SATURDAY	
I AM FEELING....	
CRAVINGS	
SYMPTOMS	
CHANGES NOTED	

SUNDAY	
I AM FEELING....	
CRAVINGS	
SYMPTOMS	
CHANGES NOTED	

MY BUMP

things to buy
before the birth

Moses Basket			
Crib			
Baby Blanket			
Car Seat			
Pram/ Stroller			
Baby Bath			
Baby Clothes			
Pacifier			
Breast Pump			
Breast Pads			
Nipple Cream			
Bottles			
Baby Sterilizer			

hospital bag

checklist

MOTHER

Maternity Notes			
Breast Pads			
Nursing Bra			
Nursing Top			
Underwear			
Toothbrush			
Toothpaste			
Pillow			
Massage Oil			
Slippers			
Socks			
Lip Balm			
Toiletries			
Clothes For Going Home			

BABY

Onesies			
Blanket			
Nursing Pillow			
Diapers/ Nappies			
Bottles			
Diaper/ Nappy Cream			
Hat			
Scratch Mittens			
Vests			
Socks			
Baby Book			
Jacket			
Car Seat			
Clothes For Going Home			

NOTES

Change Of Clothes	
Toiletries	
Cash/ Coins	
Mobile Phone	
Charger	
Camera	
Video camera	
Blanket	

ADDITIONAL ITEMS

Speakers For Music	
Birthing Ball	
Notebook & Pen	
Timer	
TENS Machine	

NOTES

birthing STORY

Example Information:
- Time contractions started
- Duration of labor
- Who was present?

25850729R00070

Printed in Great Britain
by Amazon